The Collective

Modern Epistles of Grace

Purifier Publishing

Tampa, Fl.

**Filtering the Word
for God**

Library of Congress Number:

Publishers Cataloging-in-Publication Data
The Collective: Modern Epistles of Grace; by Brian Kisner
102 pages cm.
Paperback ISBN: 978-1-7373206-2-3
ePUB ISBN: 978-1-7373206-3-0

Printed in the United States of America

The Collection

Foreword

LEGACY SCHOOL OF SUPERNATURAL MINISTRY is a school of discipleship in Tampa, Florida. Christ-centered in heart, the school gives students opportunities to experience God and His ways in a unique atmosphere. We bring in seasoned pastors and ministers to give our students good teaching, which also exists at Emerge, the mother church of LSSM. The diversity of teaching and interaction creates a fervent atmosphere of the Spirit that is profoundly full of life. All challenges from finances to prophecy are borne together in their close-knit and heartfelt group meetings.

The "kids," as I call them, range from 20 to 70 in age and are an extremely diverse group of precious saints desiring to learn the ways of God. I am proud of what is accomplished in these students' lives. This book is from their hearts; each chapter is from a different student who shares their experience in life and godliness. I am confident you will be touched by their stories.

Faith sometimes shows up like a whirlwind, and that explains what all came out of this book. The school has begun a publishing company called Purifier Publishing. Our goal at Purifier Publishing is to publish books and yet maintain the author's ownership of their books while being faithful stewards of God's provision and love toward His purpose and goals in our lives.

Due to the COVID-19 pandemic, the book was put on hold in April of 2020 and is now coming to fruition in 2021. Lives have changed drastically since the writing of these chapters, but nonetheless they are the legacy and heart of those who attended.

We hope and desire that you can reap from those experiences and we present the hearts of the students of the Class of 2019-2020. Please send any feedback and testimony to the email included in the manifest of this work. Nothing but honor to those whose names adorn these chapters.

Dr. Robert Brian Kisner D.D.

Chapter One

A Deeper Place by Joy M. Wert

The day breaks and my heart longs only for You, God. My faithful Lover, my Friend. You have brought me through mountain and valley. You've carried me over the great sea. You've held my heart when I thought I couldn't even go on. My greatest hope is in You. You have rescued me from my darkness. The fear? Banished at the sight of You. My One and Only, my deepest desire. All I am is Yours. The goodness of You overwhelms my heart. Your patience with me is so vast. Your sword goes with me by day to protect Your truth within me. Your words whisper to my heart, and I am at rest.

You are my very breath, my life, my song. My whole life is built on you, my King. With every breath, I will sing Your praises. My heart beats only for you. There is no one I'd rather be with than You. My spirit cries out for You and You alone. I want to be Your steadfast love, a place where You can rest Your head. Find me faithful. Find me true. I could not go on without You. Your love flows through me like a river; it will not be stopped. No ocean could hold it, no boundary could contain it. For You, my love, it ever grows.

My prayer for you, my beautiful friend, is that you find a deeper place in Jesus' love as you read this book, that You would begin to behold Him. Find the place where no one else can go. That quiet, beautiful secret place. The place where there is no guilt and condemnation, but there is loving conviction.[1] His goodness. There is no pressure there, only love that inspires. There is freedom, pure joy. It is here that you find Love itself. A love that formed you in your mother's womb, that knew you intimately and has authored and finished your faith.[2] A love like no other. It fulfills and completes. Find the quiet rest that enables you to be the salt of the earth.[3]

> "...Go out, and stand on the mount before the LORD. And behold, the LORD passed by, and a great and strong wind tore the mountains and broke into pieces the rocks before the LORD, *but* the LORD *was* not in the wind. And after the wind an earthquake, *but* the LORD *was* not in the earthquake. And after the earthquake a fire, *but* the LORD *was* not in the fire. And after the fire was a low whisper.[4]

Find that small voice. He is always talking if only you will listen. He is talking to you while you're driving, while you're at school, while you're at work, while you're sleeping. He speaks through everything. He gives dreams. He whispers. He thunders. He speaks through books, through movies, through people.

He gives clean hands and pure hearts so you can see and hear Him in everything. To the pure, all things are pure. You can see something and either see

---

1 Rom. 8:1.

2 Ps. 139:13; Heb. 12:2, KJV.

3 Matt. 5:13.

4 1 Kings 19:11-12.

the ugly or the purity in it. Begin to see with eyes that look for Him. "For the earnest expectation of creation awaits for the revelation of the sons of God."[5] Why? Because when you begin to behold the Lamb, you begin to look like Him. To manifest His will on the earth. To walk in your identity as His child. To release His Kingdom on earth as it is in Heaven. Don't settle any longer for formulas and religious tradition. Arise and shine and behold the Lamb. Won't you behold Him? Won't you look upon the One who gave all for you? He waits for you. All day. He wakes you up just because He wants to be near you—not only to teach you and mold you, but to simply love on you. All that He has done is to reveal to you His love.

The rest of your life depends on how much you look at Him. The more you behold Him, the more like Him you become—the more like *you* you become. The fruits of the Spirit begin to grow as you behold. We were originally created in the garden in our most perfect and fulfilled state to commune with God. We needed nothing from Him because we had everything. And yet, communion was the goal. To walk with Him in the garden is the most beautiful privilege one can receive. To walk in the cool of the day with the One who hung the stars. The One who spread out the heavens as a tent to dwell in.[6] He wants to walk with you. He made the garden for you; He made you for the garden. Walk with Him in the quiet.

Father, I pray over Your wonderful one reading this, that they would be filled with the loveliest sense of Your presence. Cover their life with Your goodness, Your kindness. Let them begin to see the beauty in

---

5   Rom. 8:19, BLB.

6   Ps. 19:4b.

beholding Your face, in waiting upon You. Take them deeper into Your heart this day. Guide them into Your truth and guard them as they go in and as they come out. I thank you, Father, for the freedom and joy being released into their lives even now. Thank You for opening their eyes to see Jesus in everything, for tuning their ears to hear Your every whisper. Thank you, Lord, for lifting their head up above their enemies, that 10,000 may fall at their side but they shall not be touched.[7] Give them a revelation of Your grace today—Your grace that paid the price and is so beautifully dependent on Your unfailing goodness. I bless them, Lord, and I thank You for their life. Thank You for all they are building and creating for Your kingdom. We love You, Jesus.

Joy M. Wert

---

7   Ps. 91:7.

Chapter 2

My Journey by
Melissa Marchese

A little background on myself: My family was Catholic, but we never went to church. Even still, I would go to different churches with different friends throughout my childhood. One time when I was about ten years old, I went to a church I had never been to before. It was different than all the rest. The people raised their hands during worship, yelling and speaking in different languages that I didn't understand. I wasn't afraid of it, even though it was unfamiliar.

The preacher asked if anyone wanted to give their hearts to Jesus. My friend's mom asked me if I wanted to go up and so I did. The next thing I remember is her picking me up off the floor as I cried hysterically. I didn't know what happened. I remember how quiet it was on the ride home. Neither my friend or her mom ever told me what had happened. When I got home and told my mom, she didn't know, either. She would not let me go back. But I always felt like something special happened to me that night.

Fast forward fifteen years. A friend of mine invited me to a church, and it was just like the one I went to as a child. All the memories of that night came back to me when I was in that church. I broke down crying and didn't know why. I had gone to other churches and never had that feeling. This time I was able to ask my friend what it was. She told me it was the Holy Spirit! No one in my family understood that feeling, so the people at my church became my family. It has been difficult not being able to share things of God with my family, but I could talk about God stuff with the people at my church easily.

My journey to LSSM began when the church I attended merged with Emerge, the church that was affiliated with LSSM. My pastors at my old church were being called to another state. When my old church was gone, I felt lost, like my family had disappeared. I had heard of LSSM a few times because I knew people that taught there. When I started going to Emerge, they were advertising the school, and I went to a preview. Everyone who talked to me there was nice, and they felt like a family. I was drawn to that, and I signed up, thinking I would go for a year. I wanted to learn more about the supernatural.

It was a little different than I thought it would be. I thought, *Oh, it's a Bible college, so we are going to be learning about the Bible.* And we do learn about the Bible, but there is so much more than I ever dreamed of. The first year was so good; I learned so much about myself and about inner healing. You can't help anyone if you are a mess, and we are all such a mess. We just don't realize it until we are shown differently.

My favorite part of first year was the deliverance that we had. We call them SOZO, which is a Greek word meaning, "to save or protect from harm." I had seen in church people screaming at the person getting deliverance for the devil to come out. I wasn't sure I wanted to be a part of that. But after reading a book and having some teaching on it, I wasn't afraid of it.

It was so peaceful. I had three women in the room with me. One prayed the whole time. The second one walked me through the SOZO, and the third one wrote down what she was hearing from the Holy Spirit. I got healed from a grudge I held onto. I was in chains for not forgiving someone, and I was set free that day. You don't realize what that does to you. After it was finished, they handed me the paper with everything God said through it all. It was almost like getting a love letter from God. I think everyone should get a least one of them, even if you don't think there is any major thing in your heart. You never know what God might reveal when you open yourself up to Him healing your heart. So I was hooked. There was no way I wasn't coming back. I didn't want to miss out on what else God had for me.

I'm in my third year now and I still love it. One of the graduating seniors last year said you will only get out of it what you put into it. That is so true. I have had my ups and downs with it. Life gets in the way sometimes. But what I have seen is, God still shows up. He knows the ups and downs and He is faithful. I am glad I took this journey. I still haven't found my "purpose," but I love Jesus and whatever He has for me in my future, I look forward to it. Whatever it is, I'm sure the 4 years I spend here will play a huge role in it. I don't think anything we do to learn about Him is a waste of our time. He knows the future and He knows what we will need to be prepared for what is ahead. I can't thank all the people that have come to pour into this school and into each one of the students enough. I have been blessed by them. Thank you so much for taking the time to read my story.

Melissa Marchese

Chapter 3

Salt or Yeast by
Kelly Yoder

In class one Saturday, this Scripture came up:

> Your boasting is not good. Don't you know that
> a little yeast works through the whole batch of
> dough? Get rid of the old yeast that you may
> be a new batch without yeast—as you really
> are. For Christ, our Passover lamb, has been
> sacrificed. Therefore, let us keep the Festival,
> not with the old yeast, the yeast of malice and
> wickedness, but with the bread without yeast,
> the bread of sincerity and truth.[8]

In this case, yeast is the evil, the demonic, the yucky
stuff. If the yeast represents the malice and wicked-
ness, what counterpart represents sincerity and truth?
What is a common theme that represents the good in
the Bible? After revolving this question around my
mind, I clearly heard the answer: salt![9] The salt represents the pure, the valuable, the necessary. This is
what sincerity and truth are made of. I filed this away
as a mental note, telling myself I would delve a little
deeper another time.

---

8   1 Cor. 5:6-8, NIV 1984.

9   Matt. 5:13

On the following Wednesday, the verses came up again. I started googling salt versus yeast to prove the legitimacy of this idea of opposing forces. I am no baker, but this is what I found. Salt does, indeed, retard the growth of yeast. In high concentrations, it can even kill the yeast.

In bread making, salt exerts a greater affinity for water than the yeast. It attracts the water and, sometimes, pulls it from the yeast by reverse osmosis. When salt is around in large quantities, yeast does not stand a chance—unless there is no water. If water is life, and both salt and yeast are vying for it, salt will win.

When making bread with only yeast, it creates large irregular holes in the dough. This is what Satan likes to do to us. He wants to puff us up. Make us rise too quickly. Poke holes in who we are with lies and deceit. This growth, appearing to be real, may look good as it is rising larger and more quickly than others, but in the end, it will collapse all over itself. So how can you detect the yeast? If you look at yeast, it closely resembles bread. It's the same color and almost the same texture as it is mixed in. It is only in the rising that it is exposed.

Salt tightens the structure of bread. We all need tightening, conditioning, and strengthening. It is what helps the body stay in tip-top shape. No one wants a flabby body or overgrown bread. The connection of this salt and yeast within is a parallel between actual food and the Body of Christ. He is the Bread of Life, and He is the one that brings the sustenance into our lives. When we walk in righteousness, sin does not thrive. If there is sin in a place, and we, the salt of the earth, surround it, it will die. Christians need to eradicate anything not of Christ Himself. We must be salted with fire. Dig up that valuable salt. It is who you are. You are sacred. You are part of His covenant. There were literal salt covenants in ancient times. If we are the salt, we are a part of the covenant between Heaven and Earth. If we are the salt, we bring out the flavor of the Sacrifice. Jesus gave His life as this for us. Jesus was the Sacrifice; we are the covenant! We are to preserve His great works even today. Our covenant is one of endurance. In a covenant, both parties are willing to hold up their end of the bargain, regardless of what the other person(s) do. This is how great our God is! He is always willing to keep His promises.

Sometimes we just need to unearth them. The promises are not originated here anyway. We should mine this earth for the treasure, for the salt, for anything of value. Where the treasure lies, we should be wishing to yield anything for. "The Kingdom of Heaven is like treasure hidden in a field."[10] When salt is mined from underground, it is brought forth in large units to be crushed. Much like salt, we can be beneficial to those around us as we are crushed. Extract the useful, let the rest evaporate. Then sprinkle those grains of wisdom around. Infiltrate those areas that need more of the flavor of Christ. Bring balance into the places of life that have gotten awry.

Salt is a source of health and life. It is necessary for the regulation of fluids in the body. It is also essential for nerve and muscle function and is involved in delivering nutrients. Christians are the deliverers of spiritual nutrients worldwide. We must have salt among us. As the salt, we act as messengers of the Spiritual Body, relaying things from the Father to one another. We emit electrical impulses from Heaven to those around us. With Christians acting as salt, the

---

10   Matt. 13:44a, NIV 1984.

Body of Christ will thrive to the apex to which we are called.

There is yet another example of this in the physical world. In the human body, we have blood flowing through our veins. Much like the salt does to yeast, the white blood cells also target infection. They protect the body from any foreign invaders. White blood cells restore the balance to our bodies, as we are to reinstate the makeup of the Spiritual Body. I can just picture a great army of white coming forth to conquer any growths encroaching upon us. Take your places, Light Ones. Make that which is unclean clean. Bring the state of Perfection closer to proximity. The white troops gain more ground. The Pure Soldiers take up swords and fight. As we become more like Him, our granules appear larger. Little circles of white making the mark on targets of this world. We can be an effective retainer of His goodness. We can be true through and through.

Each of the worlds is a mirror of one another. The laws are true both spiritually and physically. Perhaps we are living in a world that is less real than the one that is not readily seen. Be mindful of how what we do physically affects what we are able to do spiritually, and that what we do spiritually is influential to the physical world we live in. These concepts need to be ingested and applied.

When this word was revealed, I could only contain the zest of excitement. I thought we had something new, me and God. During the research, I realized this concept was not new at all, physically or spiritually. I guess there really is nothing new under the sun. However, it was new to me. And it came from Him. I had to learn more, but it is now my word. It may have been the word of someone else first, but when I put in the time to find out what exactly it meant, it became part of my relationship with Him.

I considered writing on some novel idea, some area of my own life that is true to me. This word is true to me because it came from Truth. He is Truth, and when something resonates within, we can become an echo of His voice to the world. He would like to fill your mouth with things of Him. The price He paid in the redemption of this world holds its value. Make sure you are living in a way that is worth yours. Over history, people have often been paid with salt. When someone is considered worthy of their salt, they are said to be effective and efficient. Are we operating as legitimate preservers of His sacrifice? This is very possible by staying in communion with the One who initialized the Covenant to begin with. This is a call to Stay Salty! To live a little purer, making sure to complete the tasks put upon us. Be worth your salt. Know your worth, and once that is determined, sprinkle salt in every place!

Kelly Yoder

Chapter 4

Oh So Glorious Life by Hannah Grant

My inspiration at this point in my life is Jesus, the lover of my soul. I realize more every day that my life is simple. My call is simple: to love God and to love people. Over the years, I have had moments in time of drawing close to God only to allow distractions and lesser things take over my attention. These things led me down paths of destruction. However, because of the kindness of God, He saved me from myself each time, even in the futility of my thinking. He not only saved me but loved me so intensely that not even shame and regret could keep their hold over me.

I've never known a love like this. I've stopped running away from it because I don't feel worthy. For who am I to reject a gift that the King extends towards me? What is this gift, you might ask? Himself. He gives Himself away. So loving Him is my priority every moment of every day. I desire to become so aware of His beauty that I lose consciousness of myself. So I dedicate this chapter to my beautiful Jesus in hopes that it awakens a hunger in you to draw near to Him.

> The King who came not to be served, but to serve His creation.

> The King who humbled himself even unto death for the sake of love.

The King who came knowing He would not be recognized by His own.

The King who loved with no agenda.

The King who brought rest to the weary and lifted the burdens off those with heavy hearts.

He is radical, yet He is kind. He is wild, yet He is gentle. He is the One who rejoices over us as we sleep, who waits beside us anticipating our arising in the morning. Though we leave Him to have affairs with the world, He never forsakes us, and when we return, He always receives us. He is the mighty lover awaiting His bride as she makes herself ready. He desires a pure and perfect bride. Yet we only become pure and perfect by the wonderful grace that He's freely given us. Yes, all He wants of us He has given us the ability to accomplish, and how delightful it is to fulfill His desires.

He loves to hear our voice in adoration towards Him. He is a King who does not look at our small lives as trivial but carefully guides us through each season as a shepherd guides His sheep. He is our unashamed lover. Even when we fall short, He does not look away but only longs for us to come closer. He is the hoping One, the believing One, always enduring with us and continuing in perfect love towards us. With just one look into His fiery eyes, we are transformed. His meekness may be mistaken for weakness, yet it is the very thing that makes Him high and lifted up above all others. He is humility. He is love. He is righteousness. He is peace. He is joy. What more could we need? Once I tasted of His honey-sweet goodness, my appetite for all other things faded away. Once I saw his lovely face, I did not desire to look at any other thing or any other one.

My Maker, my Husband, my Redeemer, my Friend; You allowed the very ones You formed with Your own hands to crucify You that You may take their punishment. You continued to give us breath as we mocked You. You sustained our heartbeats as we nailed You to a cross. It brought You great joy to die for a creation that rejected You. You chose us that we may choose You. For I am blind, but You, precious Lord, open my eyes to see the river of living water in front of me. Then, only by Your grace am I able to walk to the river, and I could not bear to drink this water except that by Your great love, You have made me worthy. You are everything, and having the privilege of loving You is everything to me. You have given me a voice to sing out to You, for You knew that bringing praise to You is what would satisfy me. You gave me hands to serve You and feet to follow where You lead, for You knew that following You is what would bring me fulfillment. Let every moment of my life be worship to You, my sweet and precious King, for You are the only One worthy of every day, every thought, every breath, every action. I love You, Jesus. Thank You for loving my soul so strongly that it caused me to arise from my slumber and be awakened to life with You, which is oh so glorious.

Hannah Grant

Chapter 5

Don't Believe the Lies
by Dan Newman

Let's talk about the lies that we all have been fed by the world. For some of us, those lies were planted by our parents, the people we trusted the most. For others, those lies came from our friends, those we wanted to be the most like. In some cases, we allowed lies from those we don't even have a relationship with to take hold in our mind. These lies cause us to find ourselves either in a performance mode to change what those lies say about us, or in a state of despair as we succumb to the inevitable results because we chose to make them a part of our core beliefs.

Why is it so hard for us to believe the best in ourselves? Why do we need to constantly remind ourselves of who we are in Christ? I believe that not only do we need to die to the flesh because of its desires, but we need to die to flesh to remove the lies that we have been conditioned to believe about ourselves.

Galatians 2:20: "I have been crucified with Christ. It is no longer I who live, but Christ who lives in me. And the life I now live in the flesh I live by faith in the Son of God, who loved me and gave himself for me."

So, if we are no longer the ones who are living, then why do we still lean toward our own understanding? Unless we seek out the truth in the word and time with the Holy Spirit, then our own under-standing is fed by things of the world.

One of the ways we can begin to drive home the truth of who we are in Christ is to express daily decla-rations over ourselves. Daily declarations are a good way for us to die to the flesh, because as we become awakened to the lies that we have believed, we need to replace them with the truth by daily reprogram-ming our brain into that of the mind of Christ.

Luke 9:23 (KJV): "And he said to *them* all, If any *man* will come after me, let him deny himself, and take up his cross daily, and follow me."

It is something we must do daily, because we live in the world and we are surrounded with a fleshly body that, left to its own devices, would seek after the things of the world. For each of us, the walk to re-place the lies that we have believed will be different.

Becoming self-aware of our character and why we react the way we do is an important step in being mature in Christ. We sometimes tend to compare our-selves with others or think we are different because we don't deal with things the same way others do. Understanding who we were made to be provides us with the power to recognize lies about who we are, and understanding not only ourselves better, but those who we interact with. Lies we believe can ham-per our ability to forgive ourselves and to forgive oth-ers. So, my challenge to you is to ask the Holy Spirit to reveal the lies that you have believed and to bring them to the surface so that you can replace them with the truth that God has for your life.

Psalm 139 23-24 (NKJV):

> Search me, O God, and know my heart;
> Try me, and know my anxieties;
> And see if *there is any* wicked way in me,
> And lead me in the way everlasting.

Once you know the truth, meditate on it so it becomes one with the depths of your heart. You must think about the truth God has lovingly spoken over you, not the lies the world has spoken over you.

> **Proverbs 23:7a (NKJV):** For as he thinks in his heart, so *is* he...

I pray that you seek to fill your heart with the love of Christ. It is through this love that you will find peace and healing in all things. It is also with this love in your heart that you will be able to release the calling in your life that God has for you. You are a child of the Most High and He has plans for you. Arise and go forth with the truth that can be found in the Word and spending time with the Holy Spirit. I declare this to be a season of truth in your life. Be free of the lies!

Dan Newman

Chapter 6

Who I Am Declarations by Dave Royal

Merriam-Webster's definition of identity states "the distinguishing character or personality of an individual."[11] It is who you are, the way you think about yourself, the way you are viewed by the world, and the characteristics that define you.

My identity is in Jesus, in how He sees me, and in my personal relationship with Him. This relationship is the greatest one you can have.

> And so I declare:
> I am created in God's image.
> God planned my destiny before I was born.
> I am a child of God. He loves me deeply.
> I have been created to worship God.
> I have been adopted to sonship through Jesus.
> I am God's special possession.
> My body is a temple of the Holy Spirit.
> I am a new creation in Christ.
> In God, I am strong.
> In God, I am healed.
> God has forgiven my sins through Jesus.
> Jesus died for me because I am worth it.

11 *Merriam-Webster, s.v.* "Identity," accessed June 30, 2021, https://www.merriam-webster.com/dictionary/identity

In God, I am filled with peace and joy.
In God, I am powerful and loved.
God says that I am wonderfully made and worth it.
I am light in a dark world.
I am both a saint and a servant.
Through Jesus, I am victorious.
I am a citizen of Heaven.
My name is in God's Book of Life.
God is faithful in keeping His promises to me.
God loved me first, so I am able to love.
God's plan is for me to be prosperous.
I have been born again by the Holy Spirit.
God has saved me through His Grace.
God has prepared me to do good things.
As an heir of God, I have a glorious inheritance.
I have been blessed with every spiritual blessing in heavenly places. I have been set free in Christ.
God created me for a purpose and He gives me direction.
God supplies all my needs.
I am seated with Christ in Heavenly places.
If God is for me, who can be against me? God is with me, so I won't be dismayed. I bring life where there is death.
God says He is always with me.
I will share eternity with God.

Dave Royal

Chapter 7

The Choice, My Choice by Lora Royal

First, I saw the dress in front of me, a gorgeous dress—radiant white and luminous silver covered in crystals and sequins with an extraordinary fullness. Then I was in that dress, but only for a brief moment. It was glorious, and then it was gone. I couldn't keep that picture of myself in that dress because I had a past that made me unworthy to wear that dress. It didn't fit me well. It was perfection, and I was far from perfection. That was then, and that was the beginning of my journey to discover who I am: God's workmanship, a royal daughter of the Almighty God. I am created in His image, purposefully made. I am washed clean by the blood of Jesus, and I am significant and unique to His calling.

My secret place used to be a cave. I didn't want a cave, but there I stood, a child standing alone, surrounded by darkness, safe and away from everyone. But once I saw that dress, I knew I had to come out from that cave.

God was calling me. I was both excited and anxious. I saw the joy others had and I wanted that. I wanted to be free of anger, free from hurt. I wanted significance. I accepted Jesus years before, but I had no idea what salvation really meant, no idea of the love rooted in salvation.

I was saved, but it took some time to realize and receive God's amazing love. Some experience His love immediately. Others, like me, struggle. It was through a painful, bumpy process that I now know that God's love is amazing and all-encompassing. The Bible, His word, declares this. Many get this once they begin to read His Word. But like me, many don't get it at first because we hear and listen to the wrong voice. I had to learn about the devil, the one who seeks to steal our identity and keep us in bondage before receiving God's love.

I used to get angry with God for situations in my life, situations in which I had no control. I blamed God for my brokenness, for the hurt others caused. You see, if God is always with us, how can He stand back and watch as bad stuff happens? One sleepless night, in anger, I asked God this very question. I cried out to Him with all my anguish. He answered me. When I envisioned myself in that dress, something inside me began to stir. Abba, my Heavenly Father, began to heal me. My true, God-given identity began to fight to emerge. His love for me—for us—is deep, and the proof is found in Jesus, the One God gave to us as the ultimate sacrifice, to wipe out *all our sin* for eternity *and to bring us back into Abba's grace.* Jesus, beaten beyond identity—like the enemy strips us of our identity. The One who conquered the grave. The One who sits at the right hand of God Almighty.

Yes, our sins are washed clean by the blood of Jesus Christ, and it is through Jesus Christ that we can have direct relationship to Father God. Through Jesus, we also conquered death, and we also sit in the heavenly realm. His Spirit is upon us, beside us, and in us to walk us through all our circumstances, both good and bad. Getting this knowledge from our minds to acceptance in our hearts is sometimes a painful process. But God is with us, holding us through it all.

The knowledge was there, but my heart was not open to receiving it. I wanted to wear that beautiful dress. So I cried out and God answered me. Once I emerged from the cave, I saw myself standing on the side of a mountain, talking with God who was hidden behind this mountain. Laugh all you want, but I saw a larger-than-life toe in a cloud of glory.

I found myself surrounded by a different set of people—some teachers, some acquaintances, and some very dear friends—all God-fearing believers in the true Gospel of love returning us to relationship with our Father.

I cried out and God answered me, renewing my mind. He declared His truth through His written word, spoken word, and music. I am one of those people for whom hearing is more effective than reading. God inspired music gives life to His Word, and opens my heart to see His Truth, and Truth becomes my reality in which strongholds and lies diminish—a process of exposing lies to reveal truth, layer by layer.

How wonderful, yet I still struggled with my identity. How wonderful that the Holy Spirit was stitching up wounds, reaching into my heart, breaking down self-set limitations—transforming me. Although I still doubted the depth of God's love, I chose to keep moving forward: More layers loosed, more lies released, more Truth received, and *suddenly* I no longer saw just God's toe! His glory appeared above, below, all around me.

His presence was and is there whenever I choose to enter it. But I still struggled with lies. One day I was filled with His joy, His peace, His presence; the next day I was listening to the other voice. Then I learned of God's grace—constant unearned favor—His gift to us. I could see this grace flowing down from heaven—a golden, constant flow of unearned favor, covering everything. Nonetheless, I still couldn't seem to grasp it.

People kept telling me, "It's all in your mind." I was tired of those words to the point of shutting down and receding back into that cave. Would this ever end? I was embarrassed by who I was and therefore believed others had that same perspective of me. But I wanted to wear that dress, so I chose to keep moving forward. From the beginning of my journey, I thought I had surrendered to God. But it turns out God removes piece by piece, layer by layer, and I had come to a junction in which I had to make a major decision: Stop listening to the wrong voice.

I cried out and He answered me: MY CHOICE. I had to choose to receive God. The Holy Spirit will transform us so far, but there are some things we need to consciously choose. I finally made the choice to receive God's love, to see from His perspective and to discard the lies the fallen one tosses at me. "…[G]reater is He that is in you, than he that is in the world."[12] God created everything, including the fallen one, and God is all-powerful. I chose God, and suddenly grace was no longer limited to a cylindrical flow...I realized that grace is a glorious, constant flow all about us.

His love is so bountiful; it fills us *if* we choose to receive it. Love is God's nature; we cannot earn it.

---

12   1 John 4:4b, KJV.

From the beginning God wanted relationship with the people He created in His likeness. "So God created man in His own image; in the image of God He created him; male and female He created them."[13] Through my journey, I wanted the dress to fit me in all its perfection, but felt so imperfect that I could not receive that gift. But God created that dress, and I was the one needing alternations to wear it. If I had seen myself as God sees me, that dress would have been a perfect fit even before my transformation.

It is interesting that the Complete Topical Index in *The New Strong's Expanded Exhaustive Concordance of the Bible* defines "dress" in the following manner:

To prepare something, to:	
Cultivate land	Genesis 2: 15
Trim lamps	Ex 30:70
Prepare foods	Heb 6:7
Become presentable	2 Sam 19:24[14].

I never had to convince God of my worthiness to wear that dress. I never had to work for that dress. The only cost was a decision to listen to His voice and rebuke the other's voice. During this journey, the Holy Spirit was healing soul wounds. Jesus invites us to His table. When we accept His invitation, He cleanses all our sins, forever forgotten.

Lora Royal

---

13   Gen. 1:27, BSB.

14   James Strong, *The New Strong's Expanded Exhaustive Concordance of the Bible,* Red Letter ed. (2010), s.v. "Dress."

Chapter 8

As a Man Thinks, So is He by Mary Olson

If I were to ask you, "What do you think the Bible is all about," what would your answer be? After all, we are talking about the best-selling book of all time. Some would answer that the Bible is all about God. Others might say the Bible is all about Jesus. Some consider the Bible to be a book of dos and don'ts. I propose that the Bible is a book about the way we think.

The Evangelical Christian Bible contains 66 books written by 40 writers. You will notice that there are 40 writers of the Bible, not 40 authors. The Bible is a compilation of 40 writers recording their Holy Spirit-inspired impressions through the lens of their perception. These writers' perceptions have been rewritten in multiple languages and translations, filtering through denominational doctrines and beliefs. Words have been added and deleted to suit the present perception of the individual.

Please do not misunderstand, I believe that the Scriptures are invaluable for guiding us to a meaningful relationship with our Creator. The only true Author of the inspired Word is the Holy Spirit, who has always been and forever will be. The only inerrant Word of God is Jesus the Christ.[15]

---

15   John 1:1.

The same way the Scriptures were written are the same way they must be digested, with the help and inspiration of the Holy Spirit, our teacher and our guide. For me, once I try to put a formula or a Bible reading plan into place, I set aside walking in the Spirit in exchange for my earthbound mindset. When you think about it, what Scripture did Jesus have to instruct Him in who He was? Was it an outside study or was it an inside working? It seems to me that it was a divine connection, a *holy* union and an evolution of knowing. Jesus, who was 100% human and at the same time 100% God, came into visibility just as we did. He grew "in wisdom and in stature, and in favor with God and man," just as we should.[16] I think one of the major differences between what Jesus came to know growing up and what we come to know growing up is how to *be*. The first recorded words of Jesus at the age of twelve are, "Why did you seek Me? *Did* you not know that I must BE about My Father's business?"[17] Jesus was born into a society of doers, but He grew up knowing the difference.

Everything that exists came into being because Elohim said, "Let there be!" In His plan and purpose, there was only effortless being. When you look at the first two chapters of Genesis, the word "be" appears several times and the word "do" never appears. In Genesis 2:8, the Scripture tells us, "The Lord God planted a garden eastward in Eden and there He put the man whom He had formed."[18] The word garden is the Hebrew word *gan*, which means "garden" or

---

16 Luke 2:52, AMP,

17 Luke 2:49, NKJV.

18 Gen. 2:8, NKJV.

"enclosure" protected by a fence. [19]). The root word is *ganan,* which means to "defend," "cover," or "surround."[20] Song of Solomon 4:12 refers to a garden as His bride.

The word "eastward" is the Hebrew word *qedem,* which also means "aforetime."[21] The word *Eden* comes from the Hebrew root word *eden,* which means "pleasure, luxury, dainty, delight."[22]

While reading Genesis 2:8, could I interpret this to mean the Lord, Jehovah, the Self-Existent, Eternal God, Elohim, Father, Son and Holy Spirit established and fixed a protected enclosure, covered and surrounded to be His Bride since before the beginning of time in complete pleasure, luxury and delight? As I ponder on this further, I have always been His bride. The two shall become one, in union with the Father, Son, and Holy Spirit. Apart from them, I can do nothing.[23] I live in them and they live in me. Isn't this what Jesus came to reveal?

Some of us, including myself, did not realize our union with the Creator of the Universe. I was taught at a very early age that I had to do something to get God to be a part of my life. At the age of six, I asked

---

19 James Strong, *Strong's Exhaustive Concordance,* s.v. "Gan," accessed July 6, 2021, https://biblehub.com/hebrew/1588.htm.

20 Ibid., s.v. "Ganan," accessed July 6, 2021, https://biblehub.com/hebrew/1598.htm.

21 Ibid., s.v. "Qedem," accessed July 7, 2021, https://biblehub.com/hebrew/6924.htm.

22 Ibid., s.v. "Eden," accessed July 7, 2021, https://biblehub.com/hebrew/5731.htm; Ibid., s.v. "eden," https://biblehub.com/hebrew/5730.htm.

23 John 15:5b.

Jesus into my heart and dutifully followed my confession of faith with immersion baptism. Unfortunately, my dutiful doing did not change my thinking. I spent a lot of time and effort trying to measure up, but always felt like I could never be good enough. Have any of you ever felt like that?

Since we did a little word study in Hebrew, let's do one in Greek. Romans 3:23 says, "For all have sinned and come short of the glory of God[.]"[24] The Greek word for sin is *hamartanó*, means "to miss the mark."[25] Another word that is substituted for the word sin is "trespass"—translated from the Greek word *paraptoma*, which means a "lapse," or "deviation" from truth.[26] The words "come short" is one Greek word: *hystereo*, which means "to be behind." It is a metaphor for "fail to become a partaker" or "fall back from."[27] The Greek word for "glory" is *doxa* which means "opinion, judgment, view."[28] When the term is used in the New Testament, it always refers to a "good…opinion" concerning one, resulting in "praise, honor, and glory." While contemplating Paul's statement in Romans 3:23, I could understand it to say, "All have missed the mark and deviated from the truth, which hinders us from fully partaking of what God's view, opinion, and judgment has

---

24 Rom. 3:23, KJV.

25 Ibid., s.v. "Hamartanó," accessed July 7, 2021, https://biblehub.com/greek/264.htm.

26 Ibid., s.v. "Paraptóma," accessed July 7, 2021, https://biblehub.com/greek/3900.htm.

27 Ibid., s.v. "Hustereó," accessed July 7, 2021, https://biblehub.com/greek/5302.htm.

28 Joseph Henry Thayer, *Thayer's Greek Lexicon*, s.v. "Doxa," accessed July 7, 2021, https://biblehub.com/greek/1391.htm.

always been of all mankind, which are created in His image and likeness."

Let's look at the verse following this one and see if this fits. Roman 3:24 says, "...being justified freely by his grace through the redemption that is in Christ Jesus."[29] Who is justified? All! What does "justified" mean? I found these explanations: "to declare guiltless" and "acceptable" by God.[30] Freely by His Grace! This means no one can buy or earn it. Objectively, justification belongs to all, but you cannot benefit from something you don't believe you have.

This verse tells us that justification comes to us through the redemption in Christ Jesus. "Redemption" is a very interesting word. The first part of the word is "*apo*," a preposition indicating "origin," and the second part of the word is *lyton,* meaning "ransom of a life."[31] In other words, the redemption that is in Christ Jesus is found in His incarnation, that reveals our origin.

Paul wrote in 2 Timothy 1:9, "He has saved us and called us with a holy calling, not according to our works, but according to His own purpose and grace, which was given to us in Christ Jesus before time began."[32] Our God is LOVE! Nothing can separate you from Love.[33] There is nothing you can do that can

---

29 Rom. 3:24, KJV.

30 Joseph Henry Thayer, *Thayer's Greek Lexicon,* s.v. "Dikaioó," accessed July 7, 2021, https://biblehub.com/greek/1344.htm.

31 Ibid., s.v. "Apo," accessed July 7, 2021, https://biblehub.com/greek/575.htm; Ibid., s.v. "Lutron," accessed July 7, 2021, https://biblehub.com/greek/3083.htm.

32 2 Tim. 1:9, CSB.

33 Rom. 8:38-39.

make Him love you more, and there is nothing you can do that can make Him love you less. He loves you because that is Who He is!

Jesus came to earth for two very important reasons. He came to reveal His Father—Our Father—to us and reveal our true selves to us. His message was very clear. Change your thinking! We continue to misunderstand and try harder to be more like God in our own efforts. That's exactly what happened to Adam and Eve in the beginning. Their good intention was to be more like their Creator but, to their own detriment, they forgot who they already were. By ingesting the fruit from the tree of the knowledge of good and evil, the God Sense within them became veiled. What do you get when a spirit being created in the image and likeness of God gets a taste of dualistic thinking? It gets replaced with a bunch of upside-down nonsense. We were never created to be a thought factory, and we certainly were never created to judge good and evil. The Scripture teaches us in Philippians 4:8, "...whatsoever things are true, whatsoever things are honest, whatsoever things are just, whatsoever things are pure, whatsoever things are lovely, whatsoever things are of good report...think on these things."[34] I Thessalonians 5:18 exhorts us, "In every thing give thanks: for this is the will of God in Christ Jesus concerning you." Philippians 4:4 encourages us, "Rejoice in the Lord alway: and again I say, Rejoice."[35] These are not suggestions we need to work on. This is who we were created to BE!

We are not human doings, we are spirit beings created in the image and likeness of God. "God was in

---

34 Phil. 4:8, KJV.

35 Phil. 4:4, KJV.

Christ reconciling the world to Himself," not counting people's deviation from the truth against them.[36] Jesus said, "Father, forgive them; for they know not what they do…"[37] and He only said what He heard His Father say.

It is time for us to change our minds and stop living from appearances. It is time to believe that It IS FINISHED! It is time to believe we have already been given every spiritual blessing in the heavenly realm because of our union in Christ. Romans 12:2 tells us not to be conformed to this world, but to instead BE who you were created to be by living from your union within. The Lord is my shepherd, and He leads me beside the waters of reflection, where my soul remembers who I am again.[38] You and I are God's dream come true! Stop being fooled by the lies of the illusion of your natural senses.

I have heard it said that it is all about Jesus. I have good news! Jesus is all about YOU!!! It is time to wake up! Dismiss every thought that tries to scream louder than the goodness of God! It is HIS goodness that will continually lead you to change your mind about Him and yourself again and again. You were created by Love, for Love, in Love, to BE LOVE and LOVED! Simply BE-lieve!

Mary Olson

---

36 2 Cor. 5:19, NKJV.

37 Luke 23:34, KJV.

38 Ps. 23.

Chapter 9

God Trusting Me (and You) by Stanley Christopher Burns

The love that God has for me is always worth remembering, but somehow it is still possible to forget. This love is a tremendous comfort and brings indescribable peace. It can also overwhelm every part of my being. I never want to be offensive toward Him. And because of that, there is always a question that is never far from my mind or heart. Can God trust me?

I really, really need to be in His face to do this, and I drop the ball more often than I care to admit. I need to recognize and remember that I need God in order to be obedient to him. That can only happen if I watch and follow Him. There are all kinds of things that I wouldn't trust myself with that God gives me access to. Why? Lord, what do you want me to do with them? What do you want me to say to him? Or pray for her? Or be for You?

I am in my third decade of internal challenge in this matter. Somewhere in the 1990s, I got this revelation that when He was pressing upon me to pray for someone's health, relationships, or finances, He was actually trusting me with that person to show His love to them. Yes, He was trusting me with His Word, power, and authority. He was even trusting me with a disease, an abuse, a crime, or an environment. He was trusting me with an assignment, a mission, or a task. Why would He trust me?

There is a justice from God that is loaded with mercy for the purpose of redemption. God wants to redeem things that I don't care to have redeemed—unless I keep looking at Him. So I try to keep looking at Him, because He keeps trusting me with these things. He trusts me to do what He wants to do with them and not what I think should be done with them.

Jesus Himself tells us, "Love your enemies."[39] Really? "Bless those who curse you." For real? "Do good to those who hate you." Does Jesus actually, mean this? "And, pray for those who spitefully use you and persecute you."[40] Wow! He is trusting me to be this way with people like this? So I ask myself, "Who can God trust me with?" Or, who can God trust you with? If I were in Daniel's shoes, could God trust me to be what Daniel was to Nebuchadnezzar, the guy who decimated his nation and family, then enslaved and castrated him? Could God trust me with that guy? Then there is the case of Ananias, who received Saul, the Christian killer, and prayed for him. Saul was on an assignment to do away with people like Ananias. Or you. Could God trust me with a Saul before there is substantial proof that he has been reborn?

I need to see through His eyes, hear through His ears, think with the mind of Christ, believe through the all-knowing heart of the Father, say what He says and do what He does. I need to pay attention to how He loves people. I have to listen to what He says about someone, because I really don't know who someone is unless He reveals it to me. And, even if

---

39   Matt. 5:44, NKJV.

40   Ibid.

He doesn't reveal who someone is to me, He may still entrust them to me.

Who are the people I put between me and my obedience to God? When I do that, I tell myself I don't have to obey the written Word of God concerning them because they are wrong or bad or wicked, because we have opposing views, beliefs, and politics. I can ignore the voice and command of God when it comes to them, because they are not my kind of people. When we do this, we address these kinds of people, situations, and even right principles as principalities that we have placed higher than God Himself.

When I don't sense His lead, He is still the Lord of my obedience to what He has already said. Love my enemies and "pray without ceasing" for all peoples and all in authority.[41] Not just the ones that I'm ok with, but the ones that Jesus died for. He has way more vested in them than I do. Don't be fearful. Can God trust me to speak up when He wants me to if it's not popular. Can He trust me to zip my lips when my heart, mind, mouth, and emotions are loaded with words that are pressing to get out? In other words, can God trust me with a secret? Or do I become a blabbermouth and abuser of His confidence in me?

His love toward me is so great! But not greater than His love toward others that He is trusting me with. Yes, murderers from every socio-economic background are on the heart of God, and His plan for them is not always to lose a lawsuit or go to prison. That's my plan, but He's not trusting me with my plan. The Lord has in the past, trusted me with every kind of criminal, domestic abuser, child molester, crooked politician, debauched minister, atheist,

---

41   1 Thess. 5:17.

gender-confused, KKK member and racial hater, and pagan. On at least one occasion, God brought me to someone who was partially responsible for the deaths of hundreds of thousands of people. He has sent me to mentor, pray for, and advise corrupt cops, abusive public safety officials, and destructive doctors. My testimony is that God is faithful, that Jesus died for all and the Holy Spirit restricts no one from the Father's desire for all to be saved.

King David wrote about the wicked in Psalm 36:1-2: "An oracle within my heart concerning the transgression of the wicked: there is no fear of God before His eyes. For he flatters himself in his own eyes, when he finds out his iniquity and when he hates."[42] The verses that follow these, continue to describe the duo of pride and hate and their relationship to one another. While the saved, children of God, are not considered to be the wicked, we never lose our freedom to choose to conduct ourselves as the wicked do. So the love choice has to be actively pursued if we are to choose righteously.[43]

Even God's definition of the word "hate" is to be accepted over our own feelings, definitions, and cultural norms about it. The Lord calls things "hate" that we mask under other categories. Jealousy, rage, arguing, sulking, mocking, teasing, jesting, debating, gossiping, and apathy can all end up under the hate banner of pride, or the pride banner of hate. Anger, righteous indignation, self-pity, and truth telling can be found on that long list with many others. But it is the allowance of a deep work of His love that lifts every mask on the list and lights up any darkness

---

42 Ps. 36:1-2, NKJV.

43 1 Cor. 14:1.

behind it. When I encounter the people God loves in thought, prayer, conversations with others, or communication with them directly, the removal of any mask that I have should reveal the love of God in one way or another.

Love is at the center of this trusting relationship between me and God. There is no good reason to not trust God because His perfect love is packed with and backed by all power. But Christ has placed the measure of my love toward Him in two streams that flow together. One is our obedience to him.[44] The other is our heart toward others. It is revealed, repeatedly in 1 John 4 that not loving others is not knowing Him.[45] Sometimes, I wish He hadn't said it, but He did.

We don't have an argument that can justify a lack of love on our parts in Him. He knows the truth about us. Without condemnation, He allows the conviction of my heart for my own good and for the good of the relationship that I have with Him. Yes, He is the Healer and He heals our hearts with His. Any other issue in trusting Him that may be partnering with fear is cast out by His kind of love. When God wants to use me, I want to show Him that I am available for Him to use. After all, with whatever or whomever He is entrusting to me, He has not desired that I should steward without Him. He asks me to remain in Him, and that is my desire.[46]

Stanley Christopher Burns

---

44   John 14:15.

45   1 John 4:7-20.

46   John 15:4.

Chapter 10

Come Away By
Elizabeth Barber

As I bask in His presence, my tongue is the pen of a ready writer.

Silence, my soul. Rest in Him.

Fill the air with Your presence, God. Surround me. Permeate me.

My heart longs for You, for a quiet wilderness, or a thousand-mile beach line, to feel Your presence. I feel the sand in my toes as the water laps at my bare feet. The draw of the water around my feet pulls me closer to You. Closer to abandon and deeper into You. You breach my walls, and I lose all my cares, worries, and priorities in light of Your presence. *I welcome you in*, You say. *Come in closer.*

The tears begin to fall down my cheeks. All the pain I have been holding releases its hold on me. I'm finally safe in the security and peace of Your love. Love like a warm, comforting hug encompasses my being and penetrates to the depths of my soul. I can finally let go. I can finally breathe. Finally, free.

How did I get to this place, where I thought I had to carry so much? Why don't I just stay here in this place of love, peace, and abandon? In this place, I want nothing more. It's You my heart longs for. The wind, the waves, and the sky all speak of Your goodness.

I hear You say, "Come away with Me. Let Me restore your soul. Share your heart with Me. I long to be with you, too. Surrender to Me. Let Me tenderly care for you. Give Me your ashes and I will give you My beauty. Give Me the mourning of your soul and I will give you joy. Give Me your heaviness and I will give you praise."

God, I don't want to hold anything back from you anymore. Be one with me. Be one with me.

Unified, I am securely planted in You. I no longer waver due to the doubt that creeps in through the distance I've allowed between us. I'm no longer content to allow anything to keep me from You. I am shored up to my Anchor. Though the winds may blow, I will not be moved. Though the earth quakes, I will not be shaken. My hope is in You. Your love is stronger than anything and I will trust in YOU.

Elizabeth Barber

Chapter 11

You are Chosen by Doug Barber

"Identity": "[t]he fact of being who or what a person or thing is."[47] Most of us have gotten our identity from our families, friends, jobs, relationships, past circumstances, accomplishments, and failures. These have made us because we have believed in them. We have given our identities away.

In the past I have called myself an athlete, a jock, a nerd, a movie buff, a failure, a dreamer, a has-been, a never-will-be, etc. None of those are who I really am. I am chosen, adopted, a child of God. In Ephesians 1:4-5, it says, "just as [in His love] He chose us in Christ [actually selected us for himself as His own] before the foundation of the world, so that we would be holy [that is, consecrated, set apart for Him, purpose-driven] and blameless in his sight. In love He predestined and lovingly planned for us to be adopted to Himself as [His own] children through Jesus Christ, in accordance with kind intention and good pleasure of His will."[48]

---

47 *Oxford Dictionary,* s.v. "identity," accessed July 12, 2021, https://www.lexico.com/definition/identity.

48 Eph. 1:4-5, AMP.

Ephesians is packed with identity. Throughout Ephesians, you can learn the truth about who you are. Ephesians 1:4-5 especially resonates with me on a deep level. I remember as a kid waiting to get picked for basketball, kickball, or some other activity. I would sit there, hoping and praying that they picked me. They didn't always pick me and the longer I waited, the lonelier I felt. I wanted to be wanted.

We all want to be wanted. It makes us feel important. When I read this verse for the first time, I reacted with excitement and pure happiness. God chose me, really! That truly is amazing! Not only did He choose me, but He adopted me! Then I decided to dig deeper into this revelation and understand what this truly means.

"Choose": "pick out (someone or something) as being the best or most appropriate of two or more alternatives."[49] He chose me before He even created earth. I must be really important to Him! The deeper I dive into this revelation, it strengthens my hunger for God, confidence, and self-worth.

"Adopt": "legally tak[ing] another's child and bring[ing] it up as one's own."[50] He legally made me His son! Because of this, my heart feels so overwhelmed with love and acceptance. My mind struggles to figure out God's love for me, and my heart tells my mind to shut up and be loved. As my mind stops, my heart opens for God to move me. As the Lord moves me, I feel love, acceptance, and hope replace my sadness, longing, and despair. As I contin-

---

49   *Oxford Dictionary,* s.v. "choose," accessed July 12, 2021, https://www.lexico.com/definition/choose.

50   Ibid., s.v. "adopt," accessed July 12, 2021, https://www.lexico.com/definition/adopt.

ue to grow in this understanding of my sonship, my true identity is breaking though the old false identity. Know that you too are chosen. We are chosen, adopted, and children of God.

Doug Barber

Chapter 12

Love: Do You Know Him? by Bao-Tran Do

Human beings are hard-wired to need, want, and give love. We are created in the image of love, and the God of all of heaven and Earth created each one of us to know Him and to be reconciled back to Him, after all. One lifetime is not enough to grasp the magnitude of just how powerful or immense the love of God is, nonetheless two pages.

Is there such a thing as being spiritually spoiled? Recently the internet has been swarming with the "Good News." Christians are being spoon-fed revelation, and it's a double-edged sword. I get notifications every five minutes because someone heard from God and wants to encourage the Body. There are E-course and monthly subscriptions to premium teachings that can keep me occupied for an eternity and a half. To top it all off, I attend a school of supernatural ministry that trains and equips students of Jesus Christ to walk in all things Kingdom and bring revival. The modern world lacks no resources when it comes to the Gospel and working miracles. Why, then, are so many of us confused when it comes to the questions of purpose and destiny? What is the purpose of miracles, prophesies, healings, words of knowledge, the ability to cast out demons, and speaking in tongues if at the end of the day, people still ask, "Lord, what is your purpose for my life?" What does it even mean to bring glory to God? Why do it if I'm going to die and go to heaven anyway?

Suddenly I see a body that is empowered and walking in supernatural signs and wonders, spewing recycled words that they read two months ago on the Elijah List. They are consumed with bringing "glory to God" when they haven't spent half the time in the word as they have on Facebook watching whatever prophetic video suits their season. I am not condemning anyone; in fact, I am speaking from experience. I've spent much of my walk pursuing and developing my gifts and seeking my own prominence in the world that I've lost sight of the "why." I can regurgitate commonly used scriptures and tell you about the times and seasons when I felt stuck. I've substituted the arms of the Father for social media attention, the most accessible nanny of all..

We are overloaded with head knowledge more so than ever before, and there is enough content out there to fake an entire move of God. The Bible is clear that we have *one* job, and that is to love. How does one love the Lord, you might ask? Love the Lord your God with all your heart, soul, and mind and love your neighbor as yourself.[51]

John 21 is probably one of my favorite chapters in the Bible because Peter makes me feel like I am not alone in my hardheadedness. Peter and the boys went fishing and caught nothing of their own effort. Jesus comes along with a better way, and they walk away with an abundance of fish due to their obedience. Later in the chapter, Jesus asks Peter three times if he loves Him and tells him to feed His sheep. Before this,

---

51   Mark 12:30-31.

Peter had denied knowing Jesus three times leading up to the crucifixion, and here is Jesus, still blessing Peter's catch for the day after he had walked away and tried to pick up his old identity as a fisherman. If I were Peter, I'd be on my face crying at this point.

God loves us so much that He not only knows our character flaws *and* loves us, He chooses us, gives us a new identity, builds up our faith, calls us to walk on water, and gives us wisdom, all for the purpose of transforming us into the spitting image of Him! Study the life of Peter and you'll see the blueprint to walking out in our true identities, purposes, and destinies.

I find Peter's walk with the Lord hysterical because of how relatable and human he is throughout the New Testament. He was weak, flawed, fearful, and faithless, as we all are. But the love of Christ radically transformed him into a man that was on fire for Christ and became the model for Christianity, the rock upon which Jesus built His church. He was loved and spent his life loving.

Feathers and gold dust are nice. Raising the dead and calling out words of knowledge will attract a crowd. But unless it's all done in love, it's no better than the occult. In a less mystical sense, I can believe in God for an empire of wealth, for a platform, for my family's salvation, but unless my motive is for others to know the love of Jesus and equip them to love others, then I am not walking out my God-ordained purpose. I used to believe that if God would bless me with all these things, then others would marvel at my life and hopefully see Jesus. I honestly say now that I was delusional. None of that matters! As long as I have breath in my lungs, I will seek to love others the best way I know how. That is through Christ that first loved me and every living person in the world.

As long as I am doing that, then my life, gifts, possessions, and influence will align and work together with God according to His purposes. Destiny solved.

Bao-Tran Do

Chapter 13

Broken Promise: It's Not the End by Kristin Ellis

There was something I had been praying about for years. In my prayers, I felt like Matthew 7:7 came alive off the page and was a part of my declaration in my lips. Over and over again, people told me things like, "The Lord hears you, and He is working," and "Your promise will come to pass." For a while it seemed like that prayer would finally be answered. Everything seemed to be coming into to place. I started school and everything was flowing along smoothly. I was excited to start my sophomore year. Then, *BOOM.* Within two weeks of school, my promise had come to a stop.

Pain and frustration washed over me, and then this unending question: *why, why, why? God,* I thought, *were You teasing me for all these years?*

I faced the reality of the end of the promise. I stepped into a state where my trust in God always seemed to be in flux. One moment I would thank the Lord for His faithfulness, and the next minute I would question His faithfulness. It did not help when we had pastors come in to visit our Monday night class for LSSM. They would continually preach that the Lord is a promise keeper. That was nice and all, but I was in denial. To me, it really was the end of that promise. I had to step aside, and not take another step forward.

I felt as though I was in a holding pattern, not just in my prayers, but also work and family situations.

Sometimes my emotions would get the best of me, and I would just cry at my cubicle at work. I would have to escape to the handicapped stall and have worship music or a Bethel sermon burring in my ears. Or I would rush to get home because I just needed to have some quiet moments of worship and prayer with the Lord. I needed to vomit everything out, because if I didn't, I would have stepped into depression.

In my personal worship time, I felt the Holy Spirit so near that I could feel Him in my hands. Great as that was, I needed the answers to my questions, and I wanted them now.

At the end of four months, I felt the Holy Spirit beckon me to make a list of things I would like to have in the future. *A list?* I said. *You want me to make a list? You haven't even answered my questions. You haven't kept your promise to me.* So I put His request aside for a little while.

I was in class one day and about three of my classmates from the LSSM were talking about something, then they took a total detour. They randomly jumped to, "You know, I'm not sure why I'm talking about this, but when I was about your age, Kristin, the Lord told me to make a list of what I wanted in the future."

I just smiled. "Really, now." Though I was smiling, I was frustrated. *Really, God? This again? Were all my prayers wasted? Were they just a joke to You?* Once again, I had to run to my secret place and bring all I was carrying to the altar to remind myself He is greater than my disappointment.

I remember once when I was driving home, I got stuck in jam-packed traffic. I wasn't going anywhere. The Holy Spirit asked me, "Kristin, am I a promise keeper?"

"Yes, Daddy God, You are."

He asked me again, "Kristin, am I a promise keeper?"

"Yes." I quoted Bible stories where the Lord kept His word.

He asked me one more time. "Kristin, am I a promise keeper?

"You know," I said, "honestly, I don't think You are. Because it is the end of what I was praying for, and I cannot step any further. I thought the verse You gave me was to back up what I believed for. Why did you stir my hopes up? Why?" The Holy Spirit just remained quiet and allowed me to cry out.

And then I allowed His truth into my mind. *Just because what you wanted didn't work out for you,* He told me, *does that mean I am not who I say I am?*

All at once, it hit me: I had allowed myself to let my emotions dictate my precious Father's identity. I thought back to when we had activations during class. These were times when we would have to give words of wisdom or pray for healing. In those moments, I would think *I don't want to be wrong,* or *Why would I pray for healing when this promise is not happening?* And where did this all begin? From my hurt I was going through. I just begun to repeat what I was beginning to believe, and then I really let things go.

Soon after this encounter, my personal worship was different. There was a free surrender that hadn't been there before. I would praise Him and pray, "Lord, I have nowhere else to run. Lord, You can have it all. If that means my promise is in others' hands, then let them have it. If somehow those people can get closer to You through what I thought was mine, then let it be."

Soon after, I wrote out that list and began to engage Daddy God. It was fun, and I found myself joyful in this season. I found a new promise, which was the same one upgraded to what the Lord saw in me. He saw my full potential and what I truly deserved. Anything I saw through that past lens of my promise was through a weak Kristin making insecure actions to get where I thought I needed to go to get this past promise. When my lens of the Father was clear and unblemished, then my own value for myself and my future self is when the waiting, actions, and thought are lined up with the Father's true promise for myself.

I still wasn't completely free from my pain. I would remember certain events from the past that didn't even hurt me at the time, but I would get emotional over those memories, just the same. However, I remembered the truth of the Father.

I asked the Lord, "Why am I going through this?" And He did not answer me right away. One day, I sat there in the quiet detoxing from a stressful work day in front of my house. The Lord just loves to talk in those times. He said, "I wanted you to create a list, not because I don't know what you want and what is best for you, but I wanted you to see what I have already prepared for you. The reason why you are going through this now is because I want you completely healed, so when you receive all that I have in *store* for you, this promise will be suitable in any time of your life."

I have entered a new mindset. That broken promise may revisit me, but it doesn't send me spiritually off-kilter any longer. In this sleepy state, the Lord was truly working for my good and bringing everything—the hurt, tears, and anger—together to make me a greater person for a greater promise.

Kristin Ellis

Chapter 14

Spiritual Mania by Shai Bell

Do you ever get in moods where it feels like spiritual mania? Working in mental health, I know the definition of mania: an extremely elevated mood usually associated with some disorder. However, when I say *spiritual* mania there is no association with a disorder, only communion with the Spirit of the true and living God.

It's funny. As odd as this may all sound, the truly strange part is that God can be so good, and that in this perspective, everything regarding Him is amazingly awesome. When we have Him pierce our natural sphere of life, it definitely looks and sounds like something manic. Everything changes. In this spiritual space, you'll do anything to stay in God's glorious ways of joy. You don't mind how weird you look to stay this close to Him, because you realize what He has to offer is very different. If you need to kneel on the road to host Him, you don't care.

In God's outwardly expressed presence, you have a stream of consciousness that reveals how true and tangible it is that God fights for us and is on our side! Satan makes us feel that it is us versus God, that we were so carnal, we can never be as righteous as God would say we should be. This thinking leaves us constantly at war with God. In this war, the enemy sneakily allows us to identify with his side. Due to this, and the fact that we live in a world that is completely submerged in this logic and call it "reality," we need a breath of something greater and bigger to hit us. Something that falls on us and takes us into glory and outlines a new path to more. This is a place where we are so entrenched with everything not in this world. It's so sweet, you fall more in love and become more amazed at His ways. You don't stop craving the fulfillment of God in the moment; your hunger for Him becomes insatiable. This is the inspiration to do more and seek more at its finest and most pure state.

Are you able to step outside your perspective to see the goodness that still exists beyond the surface? When your inspiration is from God, you see it at work in everything. You see everything as an opportunity to discover more of God. Only when you see His inspiration in everything are you able to truly be holy. This is holy, as in, "to be like God," Who made everything perfect by design and sees things as pure as they were always intended to be. We are transformed to be like Him because when we are able to see things as holy, we begin to treat them as holy. You respond in a way that is holy. When we do this, we are truly like God, His children motivated to the works of seeking His Kingdom on Earth.

I am a street minister. I go out on the streets and I pray, minister, and bless people to offer a piece of Jesus that they have never known. In this piece of Jesus, they see that He alone is all they have ever wanted and needed. All their searching comes to a screeching end. That simple prayer in Spirit and truth sets off a new beginning they didn't even know they needed or were seeking. The supernatural becomes very tangible and "Repent, for the kingdom of heaven is at hand" comes to life.[52]

When I am out on the streets praying with people and interacting with them, I am able to find the peace of God. The peace of God is where His heart is, and when you see and feel where His heart is, you can't stop seeing it. You crave more and more and will do anything for it at any cost. You find inspiration to continue bringing His kingdom on Earth. You hear God and begin to pay attention to how He is speaking to you and prompting you to show His love in new ways. You get to be a creator and innovator like your Father in heaven. You go from wanting to just pray out on the streets to wanting to go all out, as soon as possible.

This is the spiritual space where one says, "I'm called to live in the community of the poor or sacrifice my job to take on a new role making half as much." You suddenly feel compelled to give everything to see God work honestly and powerfully. When you know you could give everything for the hope of the glory of Christ working, you would definitely think about giving up your job for it. Sacrificing obligations, relationships, whatever the cost. I can't find anything more inspiring than the thrill of being in the presence of God working in the world, everyday life. Here and now, today.

Shai Bell

---

52   Matt. 3:2, NKJV.

Chapter 15

One New Man by Lani Randall and Lolita Sagalevich

> For He Himself is our peace, who has made both one, and has broken down the middle wall of separation, having abolished in His flesh the enmity, that is, the law of commandments contained in ordinances, so as to create in Himself **one new man** from the two, thus making peace, and that He might reconcile them both to God in one body through the cross, thereby putting to death the enmity.[53]

Who is this "One New Man"? How about a Palestinian named Lani Randall and a Jew named Lolita Sagalevich? We are Christian sisters in love with Jesus, friends for life, prayer partners, and ministers, who have been healed, delivered and knit together as family. We are One New Man!

Let us explore the biblical and historical understanding of "One New Man." In Ephesians 2:14-16, the Apostle Paul described how God tore down the wall of separation between Jew and Gentile to create "one new man...thus making peace" between us and reconciling us together to Himself.[54] Therefore, the

---

53   Eph. 2:14-16, NKJV. Emphasis added.

54   Eph. 2:15, NKJV.

power of God is not expressed in division, but in His divine unity.

Starting with the early church, we've seen amazing things happen when a Jew and a Gentile come together in unity, thus operating as One New Man. When Ruth, a Moabite, married Boaz, a Jew, their descendants gave birth to King David. In the book of Acts, when Peter the Apostle—a Jew—went to visit the Gentile Cornelius and his band of soldiers, the Holy Spirit fell on all the Gentiles as Paul preached to them. More powerful demonstrations of God's power are displayed in the remaining book of Acts when Paul, Barnabas, and Silas went to the Gentile nations and traveled all the way to Rome.

In other words, when God brings Jews and Gentiles together, there is a profound historical shift that takes place. Christopher Columbus, who is believed to have been Jewish because his diary was found written in Hebrew, worked together with a Spanish crew to travel and discover the New World. Centuries later, Abraham Lincoln chose a Jew, Abraham Jonas, to be his advisor and legal and political associate. They became the closest of friends, and together helped save the United States from being torn in two.

Other examples of Jews and Gentiles coming together as One New Man include Gentiles Oscar Schindler and Corrie ten Boom, who helped Jews during the Nazi Holocaust. If Gentiles had not joined in supporting Jews following the Holocaust, the modern-day nation of Israel may not exist today, and this is one of the most important historical events of the last century!

One of the largest revivals in recent history, the 1995 Brownsville revival that started in Pensacola,

Florida, is the result of One New Man. Its leadership included Pastor John Kilpatrick, a Gentile, and Michael Brown and Dick Reuben, both Jewish. Their covenant agreement created a three-strand cord of alignment that created an unrivaled revival!

When you see God gathering Gentiles and Jews together, what follows is undeniable power and access to another sovereign move of God. This means there is more to God's glory that has yet to be seen, and Lolita and I are determined to see it manifest on earth as it is in heaven. As we continually awaken to who we really are, we cannot forget our history, nor His story, that led us to become One New Man.

Back in 2013, Lolita and I met in a church, and the rest is His story. We felt a unity and connection with each other that led us to bond like soul sisters. Born by the Spirit of God, we were both desperate to see heaven invade our circumstances and our families, including our past, present, and future generations. And yet we needed so much healing and deliverance in our own lives. As our friendship deepened, so did God's supernatural graces.

Our personal paths to healing and deliverance started with obedience to the Spirit of God. The Holy Spirit was calling us to attend schools together, mainly for training in healing ministry, which included deliverance for ourselves and our generations. Some of our most memorable healings took place while praying over generational hatred between Arabs and Jews, and repenting for the division and strife that continues between them to this day. That strife certainly surfaced in each of us as we went through numerous ups and downs in our relationship. It wasn't an easy journey, and as painful as it was between us at times, God's pruning was necessary to get us where

He needed us. Yet we never gave up praying and reconciling to each other!

Not only did God heal us and our generations deeply, which continues to this day, but He also provided financially for these two housewives living on a budget. At one point, we just didn't have the financial means to attend a particular school that the Holy Spirit was leading us to attend. Suddenly, we experienced supernatural provision when one of us received a check in the mail for thousands of dollars from a fifteen-year-old pension that was never redeemed! It happened to arrive just when we needed tuition for the next school! Needless to say, God makes a way where there is no way!

Aside from our schooling, we were blessed with opportunities to meet people of different ministries who spoke into our lives and prayed for us. Neither Lolita or I grew up knowing much about all the different Christian ministries that existed, nor did we grow up understanding prophetic words. However, we were honored to receive prayer and prophetic words from many of the ministers we've met on our journey, some well-known and some not so well-known. One particular minister who made a huge impact on us was Matt Sorger of Matt Sorger Ministries. On one occasion, Matt blessed us and called us One New Man. That is when we officially received the revelation of One New Man and its significance. Furthermore, Peter Horrobin, founder of Ellel Ministries USA, taught us that when Jews and Gentiles pray together, the power of God is released.

As a result of this revelation, Lolita and I would get together and pray on numerous occasions for breakthroughs in our families and with friends. The testimonies have been incredible for both of our fam-

ilies, and too numerous to count, but we started recording our experiences as we continued expecting
God to move. One of our biggest breakthroughs came
when Lolita's eighty-three-year-old Jewish father accepted Jesus and converted to Christianity! After we
prayed, his heart was ready to receive Jesus as Lolita
brought him to Christ.

A big testimony for my family is that there used to
be so much division, but having prayed with Lolita,
we've witnessed my family members forgiving each
other and reconciled after years of tension and division. The generational unity taking place is so powerful that God has opened up communication lines between me and a cousin who loves the Lord and who
lives in a neighboring suburb, and yet we've never
known about each other until a divine exchange took
place on Facebook. I also recently found out that I'm
related to a well-known family whose healing ministry, miracle services, and global evangelism are
known world-wide. All these years we've been "dis-
connected" until now!

One of my favorite testimonies is when Lolita and
I and another friend of ours prayed together for a baby
who tested positive twice for Down's syndrome. The
mother was related to a friend of mine who used to
be Muslim, but converted to Christianity shortly after
we met. My friend, a "baby" Christian, had faith that
Jesus could heal the baby, and so we prayed expecting God to move. Sure enough, the third test came
out negative. God healed the baby in the womb from
Down's syndrome! Just when we thought the battle
was over for this baby, we found out the mother had
an infection towards the end of her pregnancy and the
baby developed water on the brain. The doctor was
encouraging an abortion, but we knew God would

move again and He did! Mom and baby got healed through prayer and he's now a very healthy young boy. I get pictures from time to time as my friend, calls him our miracle baby.

We saw God move once again in 2019. After his conversion, Lolita's father started praying with us for repentance for each other's differences, repentance for the disunity, and differences between Jews and Gentiles and between Arabs and Jews. While we prayed, Lolita's father, who is a gifted seer in the spirit, had a beautiful vision of the gates of New Jerusalem open and Arabs and Jews pouring into this city in UNITY! Approximately two weeks after praying this together, CBN News released the testimony of a former ISIS leader (whose name remains anonymous for safety reasons) who converted to Christianity because he encountered God's love in a dream. He testified, saying, "I saw a love didn't exist in Islam!"[55] His miraculous transformation was reported by Dr. Michael Youssef's Leading The Way Ministry, whose mission is to touch the most unreachable lives in the Arab world.[56]

In conclusion, Jesus broke down the barrier dividing the two to create "One New Man" in which there is peace and reconciliation. In the fourth century, John Chrysostom, Archbishop of Constantinople and early church father, described Jews and Gentiles as "two statues, one of silver, the other of lead," which

---

55 Jones, Ericah. "Former 'Prince of ISIS' Turns to Christ After a God Dream: 'I Saw a Love That Didn't Exist in Islam.'" *CBN News*, March 16, 2019, accessed July 13, 2021, https://www1.cbn.com/cbnnews/cwn/2019/march/former-prince-of-isis-turns-to-christ-after-a-god-dream-i-saw-a-love-that-didnt-exist-in-islam.

56 Ibid.

are then "melted down" to produce one new golden statue. In the last century, Martyn Lloyd-Jones, an influential Welsh Protestant minister, insisted that the church is "not a mixture of Jew and Gentile, but a new man...a new creature" based on 1 Peter 2:9-10. Likewise, Harold Hoehner, an American biblical scholar, translates Paul's One New Man as "A new race that is raceless!...They are not Jews or Gentiles, but a body of Christians who make up the church." Yes, we believe WE are this new race!

There was nothing sudden about Jesus' first coming as a child born to Mary. The "suddenly" message pertains to our generation and is an introduction to Ephesians 2, as we believe the true Messenger of the covenant is returning, only this time, He is going to come suddenly. We must be ready. When Jesus returns, we will be as ONE, Jew and Gentile, parent and child, generation and generation, walking in the fullness of both covenants. Glory to God!

Lani Randall and Lolita Sagalevich

Chapter 16

The Smile of God by Diana Torres

God smiled to us

When He gave to us Jesus.

He smiled when He said,

This is My beloved Son with whom I am well pleased.

God smiled to us

When on the day of Pentecost

The one hundred and twenty people

Were baptized with the Holy Spirit.

God smiles to us

When we accept Jesus in our hearts,

When we help a person in our prayers,

When we help the widow and the orphan.

God smiles when we open our eyes to Him,

Knowing that the creator of heaven in earth is our Father.

We carry His DNA. The closer we get to Him,

The happier and more secure we are.

When we walk in holiness He smiles!

God smiles to us

When He always makes our hearts blessed.

God smiles when we are the mirror of His Love to the world.

Proverbs 15:13 explains that a joyful heart makes a cheerful face.[57]

Sometimes we are too busy or preoccupied to fully realize His smile on us!

Like a mother expecting a child,

Preparing, loving, and smiling for the new baby

Is how God loves us and smiles before we were formed.

We are His masterpiece.

Can you imagine how the Father, Jesus, and the Holy Spirit smile in the Heavens!

Diana Torres

---

57   Prov. 15:13, NASB.

Chapter 17

To Live, Move, and Breathe through Christ by Lisa Newman

As a mother of six children—five boys and a girl—learning to live, move, and breathe through Christ's perspective has been an adventure. I never knew how difficult it would be to raise a large family, work full-time, and pursue the passion within me to serve my God at all cost! As I chose to say "Yes" to God's purposes in my life, my adventure of connecting Heaven to Earth began. God has never forsaken me despite many fiery trials. It's through those fiery trials that God has taken me from one level of His glory to higher levels of His glory. I would not trade any of those trials for easier days for the sake of losing out on the revelations from seeing God's heart in those dark seasons.

We were created for the hope of HIS glory![58] We were created to reflect and mirror the nature of Christ. The script is written. The script does not need a rewrite. The journey simply requires Christ's perspective. We begin to truly walk by faith when we truly understand the magnificent, priceless love of our heavenly Father.

---

58   Col. 1:27,

Christ's love for us is endless.[59] As we transform into his nature, we will move from glory to glory here on this earth. If my purpose is to reveal the hope of God's glory, then I must choose to abide in him, as He abides in me.[60] We want for nothing when we seek Him first. All these things are added unto us![61] Our hearts and words will reflect His Heart, His voice, His words to the world around us when we live, move, and breathe as one with Him. When we are one with Him, we find our true fulfillment. We were created in his image![62] We were created with his DNA. We are a spirit living, breathing, and functioning in the flesh, just as Jesus was God made flesh. The Holy Spirit came to live in us, here on earth.[63]

To activate and implement Christ's nature within us, we simply reflect or mirror His Heart! To know His Heart, we need to maintain a personal relationship with Him. As we allow the Spirit of God to increase within us, then we move from glory to glory. Our desires and emotions transform and change towards His desires.

Life is full of disappointments. Tragedies surround us. God never said life would be absent of trials. It's a race to the finish line.[64] Living, moving, and breathing through Him creates a freedom perspective. A freedom perspective asks, "What is Your heart, God, and what is my assignment in this difficult place?" Without a

---

59 1 Cor. 13; 1 John 3:1.

60 John 15:5.

61 Matt. 6:33.

62 Gen. 1:27.

63 Eph. 1:11-14; 2 Cor. 3:16-18.

64 Heb. 12:1.

freedom perspective, we ask, "Why is this happening to me?" A freedom perspective is walking on water despite the storm. If our focus is on Him, we stay above the crashing waves. A freedom perspective develops a joyful endurance through the difficult journey.[65] A freedom perspective responds rather than reacts to life. A freedom perspective is truly Christ's perspective.

The Bible gives us tools on how to rise above your own perspective. Changing our perspective is an internal adjustment. It's a growth process. We begin to be empowered from the inside out! It's wrapping our hearts around the darkness that surrounds us so that we are standing amid the fallen thousand.[66] It doesn't mean that our hearts are not going to be broken or affected by those who fell beside us, but Christ's perspective provides the understanding that this is a temporary situation. This life is a journey. It's just a timeline. We are provided this timeline to grow, learn, develop, and come into the revelation that we are the Hope of His Glory. We are the righteousness of Christ. God's heart is that all would be saved and come to know Him!

When we allow Him to move, breathe, and live within us, the authority from His power that rests within us is enough to change the world![67] We are here to change the atmosphere for God's purposes and to thwart the enemy's tactics that destroy, distract, and delay.[68] Our purpose is to pour out God's heart into the areas we influence.

---

65   James 1:2-12.

66   Ps. 91:7.

67   Acts 17:28.

68   John 10:10.

Above all, God wants us to know His love for us. His love story writes the script of our journey when we choose Him!

Lisa Newman

Chapter 18

The Misfit & The Church by Ryan Smith

I got saved at the age of 18. Up until that point, I was a misfit and an outcast in my social circles. I was never the popular person. I was often the person that was bullied and mocked.

I found God while I was on the way to kill myself. I joined a youth group, and eventually a church. I would express my thoughts and my dreams to the church, but they were never accepted. In a lot of ways, I felt the rejection that the world gave me coming from the people who said they loved me and were in my corner.

I eventually went from the church to ministry school. I call it ministry school, but really a lot of it was indoctrinating people in religion. I quickly began to feel like an outcast there as well. These feelings led me to stop trying and just hang out with the people I wanted to hang out with. I began to isolate myself from most people.

While there were a plethora of positive experiences, relationships, and lessons I've learned during my time in the churches and ministry school, what I've found is that the majority of church leadership was only interested in what I could do for them, not in who I was. There was a lack of fatherhood. Nobody was interested in my dreams and desires. Nobody was invested in my hopes and aspirations. Nobody was listening to my heart, and that came across as not being interested in me.

The Church as a whole today is not built for people like me. As I mature and grow closer to Jesus, I'm becoming more and more accepting of that. I now realize that the rejection of the misfit in the church is the rejection of Jesus today.

We don't belong in most places. We don't fit in. It's not that we quit going to those places, it's that we understand that we aren't really accepted. What does it mean when we say, "Jesus hung out with sinners?" The sinners are the people the church rejected in that day. Think about that. We are so good at promoting our modern-day synagogues, but not so good at doing what Jesus actually did.

The misfit needs love just as much as the white-toothed pastor in his button-down shirt who is too concerned with getting his numbers up. The difference is the pastor expects love; the misfit has gotten to a place where they stopped valuing themselves enough to expect it. When the day comes that someone shows them love, they break boundaries. They crave love and affection so much that when Jesus is shown to them, they begin to violate private time. It's not that the misfit intends to do this, they just don't know how to respond. They have never been shown.

The misfit comes into the Kingdom and accepts real love. The gospel to the misfit is this: you belong. The misfit may not fit into the church, but they do fit into the body of Christ. They are needed by the kingdom. We do a great job preaching salvation and telling people they have it all after they get saved. The misfit has a part to play in revival. In fact, if we would take the time to disciple the misfit, they would become the new generation of leaders in the church. My summation is that we don't take the time to properly disciple some people because we are afraid of what would happen if people like me were in positions of leadership. We might create a group of believers who look and act more like Jesus and who go out into the world.

The misfit is the person who doesn't smell good. They don't wear the most fashionable clothes. Sometimes their personalities are off-putting. They are socially awkward. God made them socially awkward for a reason. A misfit will fall in love with Jesus and then allow Jesus to transform them while everyone else is being cliquish with each other. And we don't really like this person even in their transformation, because we can't easily control someone being discipled by Jesus.

The misfit becomes doubly rejected. Once for their personality—before and after being transformed by love—and again, because we fear what we can't control.

We are becoming a generation of people who only want Jesus. Jesus wants our generation, but he wants our entire generation. He doesn't want only the people we pick and choose. The misfit moving in the presence of God is the sign and wonder of God taking what man has counted as useless to confuse the wise.[69] Learning is great and it has value, but only if we don't let it become a tool of superiority.

---

69   1 Cor. 1:27.

Jesus was the ultimate misfit. He is still rejected today. He was born and placed in a manger surrounded by stinking barnyard animals. He was uneducated, yet taught the teachers at the age of twelve. When He was crucified, His garment was so fine that soldiers cast lots for it. He is the Misfit to end all misfits because whoever comes to Him belongs. Who are we to decide who is accepted within the walls of the kingdom?

Ryan Smith

Chapter 19

When I Fall, I Shall Arise by Joan McCann

After sixteen years of marriage, I had to get a divorce. My husband's drinking had steadily increased in frequency and quantity. When he drank, he was verbally abusive, and occasionally physically abusive as well. Even though I knew that God hated divorce, I could no longer live with both "Dr. Jekyll and Mr. Hyde." My closest friend even informed me that she had picked up my fourteen-year-old daughter walking along the road. My daughter told her she was going to run away from home. And so, I filed for divorce.

Even though I needed to extricate myself from the marriage, I still suffered the deep feelings of loss and failure. I might have escaped Mr. Hyde, but I missed Dr. Jekyll. It felt like my heart was being torn apart, but worst of all, I felt like a failure. I had failed my children, who I should have rescued sooner, my family, who didn't want me to marry him in the first place, my marriage, and even God. I kept thinking, *if only I had had more faith! If only I had prayed more! If only, if only....*

One day a few months later, I happened to open my Bible to the book of Micah. It wasn't my intended reading for the day, but as I glanced at the page, my eyes fell on Micah 7:8.

Do not rejoice over me, O my enemy. Though I fall,

I will rise;

Though I dwell in darkness,

The Lord is a light for me."[70]

The words seemed to jump off the page at me! Even though I would like to say that at that time I fully accepted that I was loved and restored, in those moments, that was not the case. However, a crack had opened up in my self-imposed darkness, and a sliver of light and hope had found its way in!

Over the next few months, every time I picked up my Bible, it fell open to that same passage. I'm pretty sure that if I had dropped it on the floor, it would have fallen open to it. But I guess some of us must have thicker skulls (or hearts) than others. Although I wanted to believe that I wasn't an outcast, it was hard to accept the fact that God would ever be able to use me again. Even so, God didn't stop sending the message.

I had recently moved to California for a new job. That summer, I was close enough to attend Kenneth Copeland's Believers' Convention in Anaheim, and I was excited. Jerry Savelle was one of the speakers, and he taught on the scripture—drumroll and cymbal crash here—Micah 7:8. As part of the teaching, he had us all stand. Then we were told to sit down while saying, "Though I fall," and stand back up saying, "I will rise." We repeated that cycle several times. It seemed so simple, but to me it was confirmation that what God had been laying before me all that time was real.

---

70   Mic. 7:8, NASB 1995.

What had been a small crack in the darkness opened up to a flood of light and forgiveness.

Since that time, I have had opportunities to share this story and scripture with several people who felt guilty for their perceived failures. I remember one woman in particular, a pastor, who had committed adultery. When I shared with her the scripture and story, she grabbed on to it like it was the only life raft in a vast stormy ocean.

I now have the privilege of being the Dean of Students at LSSM, a position I never would have dreamed possible in those dark days after my divorce. Many years have passed since I learned the lesson of Micah 7:8. During that time, I have had many opportunities to fail, but now my response is:

Do not rejoice over me, O my enemy.

Though I fall, I will rise.[71]

I am very thankful that God is patient, not giving up on us even when we have given up on ourselves. That He cares enough to keep speaking to us through whatever means necessary. That He doesn't see us as failures, but as those who will arise, triumphing through the blood of Jesus!

Joan McCann

---

71   Ibid.

Chapter 20

This is My Life by Joshua Cable

My parents are both from western Pennsylvania. They grew up in the church and have close families. They both made great choices and positioned themselves to be able to raise up a family to the Lord. When I was born, I had the same size head I do now—big! It's funny now, but growing up with a head that size wasn't fun. I remember clearly being made fun of all the time back to elementary school. I went from being in a loving home of security to a school that beat me down with words that left me feeling unwanted, ugly, and very angry.

I'm not sure if I ever spoke much of it because I spent most of my life ignoring it and forgetting it as much as possible. I do remember the one time where an older kid up the street bullied me on the bus so horribly that I did tell my parents. My parents then told the school so when the older kid got in trouble, I got it worse from him. From that, I learned not to tell my parents anything, because it wouldn't improve the situation.

I felt so alone because I wouldn't talk to anyone about it. I didn't know what to do with my feelings, so I stuffed them far down deep within me. It seemed the more I stayed busy, the more I didn't feel quite as bad about myself. I got involved in so many different sports, Cub Scouts, band, and always a part of something with church. I knew a lot of people, but never really felt like a part of anything.

One day, when I was twelve years old, I went to my friend's house for the weekend. There were cigarettes, beer, and girls. I remember the one girl downing a Mickey's grenade and then looking at me, as if to say, "Whatcha gonna do?" I had never tried alcohol before, but I knew one thing for sure. There was no way I was getting made fun of for something else in my life, especially getting beat by a girl drinking more than me. I cracked one open myself.

For the first time in my life, I finally felt free. It was like my hands all the way up to my shoulders had been clenched up for years and then all that tension released at once. All the anger, hurt, depression, confusion, and loneliness went out the window. I felt like I could breathe once again. At that moment, I thought I knew what had been missing my whole twelve years of existence. It was my solution then, and was for the next eighteen years.

Unfortunately, it didn't just stay with beer and quickly escalated farther than I had ever imagined it could. Since I saw that high as my solution to all my problems, I would eventually do whatever it took to get it. I quickly got into hard liquor and weed. I was arrested on Easter Sunday—the most important holiday my family celebrated—at the age of fifteen for public drunkenness, underage drinking, and possession. I saw nothing wrong with it, though. If they knew what I was going through, they would do the same thing. My family's suggestions of me giving it all to God were great, but I wanted nothing to do with their godly solutions. Later that year, things got worse. I was kicked out of my house and had to live with my pap.

While on probation, I started getting into LSD all the time, since they didn't test for that. After probation ended, OxyContin came on the scene. Between the ages of sixteen and twenty-one, I had an endless supply of Oxy, Xanax, Ritalin, and Percocet. It was all free. All I had to do was sell it for my friend.

After barely graduating, I landed a construction job, which put me around older guys that did the same things I did. Once winter came, I got laid off, and my drinking became much more serious. I was drinking a half-gallon of vodka or a case of beer a day, along with the pills. A town close by never carded me, so I had full access to alcohol anytime I wanted it. Through the next couple years, I started getting arrested, losing jobs, damaging relationships, and going to rehabs. I went the whole way to Missouri to a farm to try and get sober. I connived my way to leave the facility on work release, got a couple bottles of vodka, and drove around all day. On that day, I flipped the truck, almost killing me and two others. The farm gave me a second chance, but I ended up getting high and left. I moved back home and went right back to the alcohol. In my mind, if I stayed away from the hard drugs, I'd be okay.

The next seven years were truly hell on earth. I ended up living a life I wouldn't wish on anyone. I was hooked on heroin, cocaine, and anything I could get my hands on. I was in and out of jails, rehabs, treatment centers, and hospitals. I tried killing myself multiple times by injecting insane amounts of heroin and fentanyl, but I'd always come back by a miracle or by someone saving me.

I hated myself. I hated that I was still living. I hated myself for not even being able to kill myself. I was so broken and was absolutely repulsed by what I saw in the mirror. I would look into that mirror and say, "This is my life?" After eighteen years of this, I relapsed one final time. I was laying on my bed in a three-quarter house, blaming it all on God.

Suddenly, a thought came through my mind. *Grab your Bible.* So I went and grabbed it. Another thought followed it. *Open your Bible.* I opened it up, and it came open to a place where it revealed a bulletin from the church I hadn't been to in over a year. *Open the bulletin.* On the right side of the bulletin in big bold black letters, it said, "Joshua - Be Strong and Courageous!"

At that very moment I knew it was all going to be okay. I didn't know how, but I just knew it would. Nothing on the outside changed, but deep down inside, something shifted. I realized that He still loved me and was there with me in my darkest hour. I broke down crying.

That Sunday, I went to church. The pastor said in his opening statement, "The most important thing in life is your personal relationship with Jesus Christ." I crumbled. It was like the blinders came off my eyes. For once, I could see that my life was in shambles because of my choices to always put everything before God. I always put money, women, jobs, drugs, alcohol, the religion of just going to church, and the twelve-step program meetings in front of my personal relationship with God. I was blind but now I could see.

I completely broke down by the end of the service. During the altar call, I cried with every step I took. I knew how undeserving of anything I was, but I felt the closeness of His grace and love that morning. The deep in Him was calling into the deep in me and it pulled me towards Him. I asked Jesus into my heart again that day, and this time I knew I meant it.

After that day, my life became so much different. I could see God's beauty in everything I laid my eyes on. Finally, I started on a pursuit of truly knowing Him and building a true relationship with Him. One of the greatest things has been getting to know the Holy Spirit. I cannot recall any of the churches speaking about Him when I was growing up at all. When I first got saved, I had a lot of weight taken off my shoulders, but I still struggled with swearing, nicotine, porn, and sex. It wasn't until I was truly introduced to the baptism of the Holy Spirit and purposely started a relationship with Him that I finally became free of everything hindering me in my flesh.

I started my journey through the steps of recovery again, and I had such a great spiritual experience that overwhelms me to this day. I had completed my fourth step, a personal inventory, and just completed my fifth step, a confession, in the mountains of the Allegheny National Forest. I took a hike to finish two more steps and spend it alone with God.

As I was walking up through the forest with the stream nearby, I began to get very emotional and overwhelmed, like someone was following me. My brain rushed and all I could think of doing was just finding a place to sit and write in my notepad. I tried to concentrate, but the stream was so loud. I picked all my belongings up and moved downstream. There was a log at the edge of the stream, so I sat on it and placed my things beside me.

I was writing some things to God, when all of a sudden a huge bee buzzed right by me. Then it came again, right at my face. I got so mad. This was supposed to be a great spiritual moment!

"That's it," I said. I grabbed my notepads and waited in anticipation. I was going to swat that bee dead!

Here it comes! I cocked back and swung at that stupid bee with all my might, trying to hit it to hell. I missed it! To add to the frustration, one of my notepads loosened as I swung. It went straight into the stream. The grand spiritual moment now ended, and everything that came out of my mouth was not nice. I didn't care anymore so, in my anger, I jumped into the stream and snatched up the notepad and flipped through to see how wet it had gotten.

It was in that precise moment that I realized this notepad was my fourth step inventory. All the horrible things I had ever done to myself and others. My venting sessions in rehab where every other word was four letters long. Right then, God whispered to me in my ear. "I don't just want the things you want to give Me," He said. "I want to take away all of your pain. I want to give you a future and a hope! I want to give you My joy and a purpose for living!" My eyes gushed out tears, and a tremendous refreshing came all over me immediately. I was in His presence and I didn't want to ever leave it.

It's that moment that I pull from when times are tough, and I think there is no way out. It is this moment that the Creator of the universe spoke to me in such a way that it completely revolutionized who I am and why I'm here. All the Glory goes to Jesus!

Joshua Cable

Purifier Publishing
PO Box 89896
Tampa, FL 33689

Made in the USA
Middletown, DE
11 March 2022

62299349R00060